21 Days
of Love

How to Make Love a Habit

And

Get More Out Of Life!

Pamela Osborne

PAVERS
Publishing

21 Days of Love™
Published by Pavers Publishing, LLC
28211 Southfield Rd., #760152
Lathrup Village, MI 48076

Scripture quotations are taken from The Holy Bible, King James Version. Bold lettering has been added to the quotes for emphasis. Also, parentheses have been added as definitions.

ISBN 978-1-938989-05-6
ISBN 978-1-938989-06-3 (electronic)

While every care was taken during the creation of and production of the book, the author(s) and publisher(s) cannot be held responsible for the accuracy of the information or any consequences arising from it. Pavers Publishing, LLC, takes no responsibility for the companies advertising in this book or on its websites, blogs, or any other means of communication, electronic or otherwise.

Published in the United States by Pavers Publishing, LLC.

Pavers Publishing, LLC, 21 Days of Love, and Pavers Homes, Lady Leonora, and Lady Leonora's Living Room, are trademarks of Pamela Osborne.

Book cover and page design by Shannon Crowley,
Treasure Image & Publishing - TreasureImagePublishing.com

Editorial Development by Minister Mary D. Edwards,
Leaves of Gold Consulting, LLC - LeavesOfGoldConsulting.com

Printed in the United States of America
2012-First Pavers Publishing, LLC Edition

10 9 8 7 6 5 4 3 2 1

SPECIAL SALES
Most Pavers Publishing, LLC books are available at special quantity discounts when purchased in bulk by corporations, organizations, and special-interest groups. Custom imprinting or excerpting can also be done to fit special needs.

For information please email info@pavershomes.com, or call (248) 809-5121. More Pavers Publishing, LLC books can be found at PaversHomes.com.

Acknowledgements

I'd like to acknowledge God for all His goodness toward me. Without Him, this book would not have been possible. With Him, I have peace and love. Thanks to Him, I also have forgiveness. I also want to thank my family and friends for their words of encouragement.

I'd also like to thank my special friend, Minister Mary Edwards, who helped edit this book and encouraged me in many ways. I also thank Rahijaa Freeman of Creative Buds Inc., for her creative, business and marketing acumen.

Table of Contents

PART II

Love Inside

PART III

Love Outside

Introduction

Why is there another book on love?

It is very difficult to write something new on the subject of love, which has not already been written, played, and sung so much about in so many different ways. Yet, one could spend a decade researching the topic of love and still not be finished. There is relatively little we know, in spite of all of the information that we have so far about love between human beings. We do know that lasting love doesn't just continue by neglect or accident. We have to work at love to show our faith. "Faith, if it hath not works, is dead, being alone" (James 2:17).

While the work of love requires discipline, developing the habit of love makes it easier. The goal of *21 Days of Love* is to simplify your life, save time, and be more efficient in conveying genuine acts of love.

Some of us have become "robots" in our expressions of love to the point that it is not as effective as doing fresh new acts of love. Our lives are busy. We tend to do the same things over and over, without a second thought. We are often hard pressed to figure out what to do that is new on birthdays and anniversaries, not to mention an ordinary day where we just want to show someone that we care about them.

This book will take some of the thinking out of what to do in the practice of love, so that you are freer to get straight to the act. This book is unique, because we've gone a step further than just giving you a list of "things to do." It will take you through 21 straight days of love, so that by the end of 21 days you will have established the habit of love. By practicing love, as instructed in this book, you will have at least 21 days of love.

PART I

The Habit of Love

1

Love's Foundation

Charity (love) suffereth long, and is kind;
charity is kind; charity envieth not; charity
vaunteth not itself, is not puffed up, Doth not
behave itself unseemly, seeketh not her own, is
not easily provoked, thinketh no evil; Rejoiceth
not in iniquity, but rejoiceth in the truth;
Beareth all things, believeth all things, hopeth
all things, endureth all things.
I Corinthians 13:4-7

What Is Love?

This book is focused on brotherly and sisterly love, without sexual implications. It is the kind of neighborly love we would show to a stranger as well as a friend or family member. Nevertheless, brotherly love, when shared with the right person, can sometimes blossom into a romantic type of love. You never know. Showing your love in practical ways can be very beneficial to the giver as well. Also, as relationships mature, acts of kindness through love can make the heart grow fonder. This book shows you how to draw on love for added value in any relationship, whether it is on the job, in the community, in your church, or with family members, friends and lovers.

2

The Within
Turned Outward

*There is nothing from without (outside) a
man, that entering into him can defile him;
but the things which come out of him, those
are they that defile a man. ...Do ye not
perceive, that whatsoever thing from without
entereth into man, it cannot defile him;
Because it entereth not into his heart, but into
his belly, and goeth out into the draught (is
eliminated), purging all meats?
That which cometh out of the man, that
defileth the man.
For from within, out of the heart of man,
proceed evil thoughts...
All these things come from within, and defile
the man.*
Mark 7:15, 18, 19, 20, 21, 23

It's What's Inside That Counts

What you say and do outwardly is a reflection of what you have inside of you. "Inside" is, by reference, referring to your heart, mind and thoughts. If you do the "wrong" thing, it is usually from a "wrong" heart, mind or thought. This was illustrated very clearly by Jesus when he chastised the Pharisees who complained that some of Jesus' disciples had not washed their hands before eating. Jesus' point was that the real threat came from within their minds, not Jesus.

By the time we see a person's outrage or disapproval they have already made many conclusions based on their inner image of love and life.

3

Repetitions Reveal Purpose

And he left them, and went away again, and prayed the third time, saying the same words.
Matthew 26:44

Practice Doing the Right Thing By Repetition

Just before Jesus was betrayed by Judas and arrested, he went to the Garden of Gethsemane to pray. (Matthew 26:36-46) He took along his disciples to sit while he went and prayed. He prayed once and found them asleep. He asked them to watch him and pray too, so that they would not enter into temptation. He prayed a second time, returned to them and they were asleep again. He prayed the same prayer a third time. Sometimes we have to do things over and over, not just for our benefit, but also for the benefit of others. When people see your love on a consistent basis, they are more likely to believe that it is real and from the heart.

The Almighty God can say His Words only once and it will come to past. Yet, there were several occasions when He repeated Himself or asked a person to repeat an act several times. Below is a partial list:

1. Pharaoh had to experience the ten plagues before he let the Hebrews go. (Exodus Chapters 7-11)

2. Naaman, captain of the host of the King of Syria, was told to wash in the Jordon River seven times to be cleaned of leprosy. (2 Kings 5:10)

3. The Lord called young Samuel four times, while he was sleeping. (I Samuel 3:3-10)

It seems He knew that sometimes persons and nations needed the repetition of hearing and/or doing things several times. Therefore, repetition is not without precedent and purpose for living a righteous life. Repetitions are another way that God reveals and reminds us of his existence. Hopefully, by repeating something that the Lord wants all of us to do, that is love, then we will understand better what the Lord is trying to say to us.

4

How 21 Days
of Love Works

Why 21 Days?

One of the best techniques to change an old habit is to practice the new habit for about 21 days in a row. By experiencing the new behavior for 21 days, you increase your likelihood of getting used to it, thereby forming a new habit. The 21 days time period was written about by Maxwell Maltz, M.D. F L.C.S., in his classic book, *Psycho-Cybernetics*. (The book is currently published by Pocket Books, a division of Simon and Schuster. It was copyrighted by Prentice-Hall in 1960, page xiii.)

In *21 Days of Love*, you will be building a new mental image of effectively practicing acts of love. The more you practice the habit of turning your inside love outward to share your love with others, the easier it will be to give love. The more you give love, the more likely you will receive love. Also, by having help in being creative in love, you can keep the habit of love more fresh, interesting, exciting and enjoyable. Last but not least, God will notice and remember every act of love you do.

21 Days of Love in a Nutshell.

21 Days of Love shows you how to practice acts of love through practical suggestions, so that it becomes a habit, thus making your love life easier and better in more ways than you could imagine.

5

Building a Habit of Love

*Then said Jesus to those Jews which believed in
him, If ye continue in my word, then are ye
my disciples indeed;
And ye shall know the truth, and the truth
shall make you free.*
John 8:31, 32

What is the One Habit to Practice?

This book is most unique because it will cover
one habit. Just one. Not one a day, but the same
one every day for 21 days. That one habit is:
"Turning love inside out."

How do you *do*, "I love you?" Follow the
instructions for 21 days, and you will have loved for
at least 21 days. Once the momentum starts, you
are less likely to want to stop because a habit
formed is much easier to maintain. You can go
through the 21 days of love as an individual or you
can do it with a friend, family member, or love one.
You can even do it with a group or community.
Pastors, Sunday school teachers, parents and
mentors, can use this book as a "teaching aid" in
practicing love.

6

Format of the Days

So teach us to number our days, that we may apply our hearts unto wisdom.
Psalm 90:12

You will find the following information for each day:

1. Scriptures. The scriptures are a sampling of inspirational passages relating to that particular day's instructions. Consider studying the Bible on that day regarding that topic.

2. Instruction and explanation. The instruction and explanation clarify the core of what you are to accomplish on that day. It also provides inspiration and motivation to complete the instruction for the day.

3. Suggestions. Various suggestions are provided on how to complete the instruction. It accommodates examples for individuals alone, couples, congregations, small and large groups. You may use one of the suggestions provided, or come up with an idea of your own.

4. What you did. Space is provided to record what you did to follow the day's instruction. You may also record the response from yourself and the recipient of your love. You can also share your actions with others for ideas on how to have love for 21 days. Or, if you prefer, you can write what you did and experienced in a separate journal.

7

The Rules of 21 Days of Love

But be ye doers of the word, and not hearers only, deceiving your own selves. For if any be a hearer of the word, and not a doer, he is like unto a man beholding his natural face in a glass (mirror):
For he beholdeth himself, and goeth his way, and straightaway forgetteth what manner of man he was, But whoso looketh into the perfect law of liberty, and continueth therein, he being not a forgetful hearer, but a doer of the work, this man shall be blessed in his deed.
James 1:22-25

Continuing Continually

We have often heard, "Faith without works is dead." More than likely, we haven't heard as much about continually practicing good works so that we do not forget what kind of person we are, in this case, loving. If someone were to ask you, "What have you done in love for me lately?" would you have to stop and think about it for a while?

Rules to follow for 21 Days of Love:

1. You must follow each day's instructions.

2. You must follow them for 21 consecutive days (in a row).

3. If you skip a day, you must start all over at day one, following one instruction per day.

4. However, you can switch the days around within the same Part. For example, you can switch any day within Part II. Then after Part II is completed, you can switch any day around in Part III, except for day 21, which must be last.

5. Also, you can do more than one act of love in more than one Part, as "extra acts." But you cannot double up to complete the days in less than 21 days. (Remember, you want to practice the habit of love for at least 21 consecutive days for the maximum effect.)

If you don't follow a day's instruction, or skip it, do it over until you get it right. Do whatever it takes in a support system, if necessary, to get through it for *21 consecutive days.* Why? It is because you are developing a habit of love from the inside out.

If you have a friend, mate, or other family member who can go through these 21 days of love with you, that is a good move. You are more likely to stick with a new routine when you have coaches or family and friends to be part of your support system, especially if they are following the instructions with you. In fact, a group, class or church can do this together. You can do it "solo" or with others. The design of the instructions has that in mind. In our high tech world, you can go through some of these steps online, email, chat room, blog, or keep in touch by text messaging and cell phone. Just remember, anything written down, or especially communicated electronically, is subject to not only your boss seeing it, but the whole wide world. Use some discretion. Do it ethically. In this technological world, don't say, do or write anything that would embarrass you if it came out in the public's domain.

PART II

Love Inside

8

DAY ONE:
Love

And the second (commandment) is like unto
it, Thou shalt love thy neighbor as thyself.
Matthew 22:39

DAY 1 INSTRUCTIONS:
Write and say the words, "I love myself."

How are you feeling today? Good? Day One begins with prayer and thanking the Lord for loving you. Let us pray.

"Dear Lord,
Thanks for your love.
Thanks for giving me me. Amen."

Take a look at love from the inside. "The inside of what?" you may ask. Nothing comes out of us (i.e. love) unless it is inside of us (i.e. love). Put another way, you cannot give what you do not have. You cannot love, if you do not love yourself.

Love of God is perfected in love of others. Love of others is perfected in love of self.

The Love Within

Do you have love within you? Put another way, "Do you love yourself?" When you get up in the morning, take a good look at your body in a full length mirror, if possible, and preferably naked. What do you see? Do you love your curves, lack of curves and all? Do you love every pound registered on the scale? The instruction for day one is to write down on a small piece of paper (to be placed in a wallet or somewhere accessible to you all day long) these words:

I love myself. I love myself.
I love myself. I love myself.
I love myself. I love myself.
I love myself. I love myself.
I love myself. I love myself.
I love myself. I love myself.
I love myself. I love myself.
I love myself. I love myself.

Mean it when you repeat, "I love myself." If you don't love yourself, ask why. What are you going to do about it? What if you did something bad and don't feel like loving yourself today? Just say it anyway. No one is that bad that they should not love themselves as a human being. Christ loves you, so why can't you love yourself as Christ has loved you? He knew before you were going to do that "bad thing," but He still loves you. There is not a healthy person on earth that does not from time to time feel guilty about something.

What if you feel unloved? What if there are people who actually hate you? What if they have a good reason to not love you? That has nothing to do with you loving yourself. People hated Christ, but He did not let that stop Him from love.

You didn't get into the "mess" you may perceive yourself to be in overnight. So you won't likely get out of the "mess" you may or may not have created, or someone dumped on you overnight. That has nothing to do with you loving yourself today.

Fear, self-doubt, and other "immobilizing" thoughts tend to cloud the issues. Start clearing your head of those "confusing" thoughts by loving yourself. Okay? Are there any other good excuses? Love yourself anyway.

Go ahead. Get in line and get on board the, "I love myself" train. It's fun, after you really get into it. You can email or text message yourself saying, "I love myself." Spend every moment of the day saying, "I love myself." Verbalize and believe it. If you really get up the nerve, tell someone today, "I love myself."

LOVE THYSELF
Suggestions on how to complete this day:

1. You could copy the above section, "I love myself." Cut it down to size and fasten it to a 3"x5" index card for reference.

2. You can really get into this by smiling when you say it. Every time you go to the restroom, look in the mirror and say out loud, or to yourself, "I love myself."

3. Just before you eat, and while you are saying Grace, say "I love myself." When you are walking from desk to desk at work, visualize the words, "I love myself." While driving your car, tell yourself, "I love myself." When you are walking or biking, say, "I love myself."

4. If this is a group effort, everyone can say in unison "I love myself." Or you could quietly exchange personally artful 3x5 cards that say "I love myself."

5. For the techies, text message yourself, "I love myself." For the very outgoing, you can send it through MySpace, FaceBook, and blogs. Take a photo of the 3x5 card and save it for viewing throughout the day, or PDF a copy and send it to your computer.

6. Call yourself on a phone and leave a voice mail saying, "I love myself." Save it to listen to throughout the day.

7. If this is a church, you can leave your excuses for not loving yourself at the altar during prayer time. Ask the pastor to say a prayer about the freedom God had given us to love ourselves.

How I said, "I love myself" today:

9

DAY TWO:
Greet

*And the seventy returned again with joy,
saying, Lord, even the devils are subject unto
us through thy name.*

*Behold, I give unto you power to tread on
serpents and scorpions, and over all the power
of the enemy: and nothing shall by any means
hurt you.*

*Notwithstanding in this rejoice not, that the
spirits are subject unto you; but rather rejoice,
because your names are written in heaven.*

*In that hour Jesus rejoiced in spirit, and said,
I thank thee, O Father, Lord of heaven and
earth, that thou hast hid these things from the
wise and prudent, and hast revealed them
unto babes; even so, Father, for so it seemed
good in thy sight.*

Luke 10:17, 19, 20, 21

DAY 2 INSTRUCTIONS:
Greet Yourself Today

God does not want you to be boastful. He wants to take the credit for successes in your life because He is the reason for your successes. Paul cautioned Christians not to be too boastful. (II Corinthians 11:16)

There are limits on what you can say in a greeting card to yourself *about yourself* (not counting words of encouragement and thanksgiving.) Jesus warned His disciples to not rejoice over their powers in Christ to do miraculous things like heal the sick and cast out demons. However, there are a few things that you can rejoice about yourself, as spoken by Jesus (Luke 10:17-24):

4. 1. Rejoice that your names are written in heaven.

5. 2. Rejoice that Christ is spiritually revealed to you, regardless of your social, economic, political or educational status, even though it may be hidden from the wise, prudent, kings and prophets.

Once you get on the right track as to what to rejoice about, start looking at the kinds of things people frequently celebrate about themselves, like passing an exam, getting a new job, a new house, or a new mate. When you really think deeply about it, those things are nice, but they don't compare to your salvation. Nor do they compare to your spiritual guidance from God. Wisdom from God can keep you from harm's way, which kings and prophets could not see.

I know this is hard for some of you, but do it anyway. If you don't appreciate yourself enough to receive one greeting card about yourself, you may end up showing that lack of self-worth toward others. After all, why should they get a card and you don't? End any hint of jealousy right now and give yourself the best card you can afford. Place it where you can see it throughout the day. Therefore, make it special.

HELLO TO ME
Suggestions on how to complete this day:

1. Can't afford to buy one or get to a store? Copy or draft one with the words, "My name is written in heaven. Thanks Lord!" No excuses. Color it any way you like.

2. For the techie, send yourself one of the internet greeting cards from a greeting card company.

3. Text message yourself a greeting.

4. For the artist in you, create a pretty card. Write your words on colorful construction paper, and then use glue to add sprinkling glitter on them for a very sparkly card.

5. For the really outgoing, ask someone to send you a greeting card expressing how they feel about you, (assuming they like you as a person).

6. Don't know what card to buy yourself? At a church, arrange for the members to exchange greeting cards.

7. For the truly shy, write in tiny letters, "I am a child of God!" Then hide it somewhere for a day, where only you know where it is. No peeking!

How I acknowledged a greeting to myself today:

10

DAY THREE:
Be Happy

Rejoice evermore.
1 Thessalonians 5:16

DAY 3 INSTRUCTIONS:
Make A Happy Face

Good Morning! Put on a smiley face, yours. Today is going to be a blessed day. Thank your Lord, in advance.

Today, you are in control of your actions. You will not let others "push your emotional buttons." When you feel like yelling at the driver who cut you off in traffic, just say to yourself, "I'm going to enjoy my day." Or say, "This too shall pass. In the meantime, I'm blessed and will focus on the high road, not the low life."

If it will help you any, when you face life's everyday bumps in the road, just remember that as long as you focus on where you are going and not where you've been, you are less likely to have an accident. Don't get sidetracked by sideshows. Don't let the devil steal your joy.

Today, smile through it all. Not just an outward smile, but primarily smile on the inside. Mean it when you smile. To smile from the heart will radiate love for God's goodness in your life. You see, if you believe that God is looking out for you, you can't help but smile. He has your best interest at heart.

Of course, I'm not talking about catastrophic events that may occur on this third day. There is a time to weep and a time to laugh. But absent a real bona fide life changing event, smile today.

To smile metaphorically also means to not bad mouth anyone today. Do not gossip. Definitely do not curse, even jokingly, today. No mumbling under your breath. No dirty tricks or frowns. Some of us, perhaps not you, just complain like we are on automatic pilot about anything that comes in our minds, without giving it a second thought. It is like entertainment or passing the time of day. However, today, think first. If you must be on automatic cruise, select a smile, a friendly gesture. Silence is better than snickering at someone else's minor misfortune. Don't spread office rumors. Don't partake today. Just smile while you work or go about your daily duties, gleefully.

Leave the dirty dozen jokes on the big screen and smile today. Show your trust in God that He will take care of the little things in your life that irritate you. Try it. It is not as easy as you may think, but it's free. No special tools needed. It comes already assembled. All you have to do is move a few muscles in your face that are fewer than the muscles it takes to frown. So make a happy face.

Set an example for others. People see how you handle everyday nuisances, and they learn from your smile. But guess what? You also learn from yourself. As you smile throughout the day, you are much less likely to stay depressed, angry, or distracted from doing your work. You are in control of your activities of the day, because you are not allowing someone else to "make you mad." You will often follow your smile with kind words and deeds. It is absolutely amazing how holistically beneficial a little smile can be for your physical, spiritual and emotional well-being. So, give yourself and others, the gift of your smile today.

MAKE JOYFUL SOUNDS
Suggestions on how to complete this day with a smile:

1. Smile, even if you are on the phone today.

2. If you are at work, and someone comes into your office with the latest gossip, just smile without uttering a negative word. Then change the subject to a positive note or work matter.

3. If you are at home resting and need some cheering up, turn on a wholesome comedy movie or show.

4. If you are at home and your family member starts fussing about nothing significant, just smile and go about your daily tasks.

5. Church groups can take a few moments to smile on cue by the pastor. While shaking each other's hands, greet each other with a genuine smile.

6. Small groups can discuss the benefits of smiling, while smiling, of course.

7. For the techies, send a smiley face by text message or email to yourself or a friend. If you push the ":" symbol followed by the ")" symbol, some computer programs will give you a ☺. Isn't that amazing? Than enlarge the font size for a bigger smile.

Just do it...with a smile!

How I maintained a happy face today:

11

DAY FOUR:
Stay Healthy

Beloved, I wish above all things that thou mayest prosper and be in health, even as thy soul prospereth.
3 John 1:2

DAY 4 INSTRUCTIONS:
Check with Your Doctor

Take care of your body. Make sure you are current in all of your medical check-ups. For example, if you are a certain age, make sure you are getting your annual mammograms for the women and prostate tests for the men. Schedule that colonoscopy every so many years as directed by your doctor. Annual physical exams can treat discovered problems early, possibly saving your life. Immunizations, including tetanus shots, are important also.

How's that for loving yourself? No one wants to hear bad news, however, better now than later. Many illnesses caught early, have a better chance of being cured or managed. See your doctor about medical concerns. You'll rest better at night, instead of worrying about a pain or symptom not checked out properly.

Today, check your calendar and make those phone calls that you've been too busy to do. Also, check with your doctor regarding the type and level of exercise you can do.

What if you are all current today? Good. Then be sure to follow the doctor's orders. For example, take that blood pressure pill or other medications as prescribed. Make sure you are following the prescribed directions properly. Ask a family member or friend to assist you, if needed. Take appropriate supplements, as cleared by your physician. Not all over-the-counter drugs can be taken with certain medications. Not all herbal supplements are healthy for your particular medical status. It is always better to ask a medical professional first before trying to cure yourself with alternative "medicines."

There are wide-spread problems of drug and alcohol addictions. Call for help, if you have this problem. Call today. If you have temper control issues, sign up for a seminar in anger management. Don't worry about who will see you there. The people, who are not there, are probably glad that you took the initiative to do it. And the people, who attend, are there to learn something, just like you.

Luke was a physician in the Bible. When God gave people brains capable of discovering scientific medical "miracles" and cures, He intended us to use them. It's like another gift from God. We thank you Lord, for modern medicine.

Make that call... today.

A HEALTHY YOU
Suggestions on how to complete this day:

1. Call your internist or general practitioner to see when you need to see your doctor again. Write it on your calendar. Did you know that some doctors allow you to make appointments on their website, without the need to pick up the phone?

2. Find out when your next dental appointment is (usually every six months) and write that in your calendar.

3. Read up on your health insurance policy or research how you can get the best one for your circumstances.

4. Brush your teeth at least twice a day.

5. Read the instruction/information label that comes with your medicine to double-check that you are taking it properly. If you have any questions, check with your pharmacist or doctor.

6. Discuss general health maintenance issues in a small group or church gathering.

7. Check the internet regarding the latest information on herbal and vitamin supplements. Then check with your doctor before using supplements.

How I took steps to be healthier today:

12

DAY FIVE:
Eat Right

*Wherefore I pray you to take some meat (food);
for this is for your health; for there shall not
an hair fall from the head of you.
And when he had thus spoken, he took
bread, and gave thanks to God in the
presence of them all; and when he had
broken it, he began to eat.
Then they were all of good cheer (encouraged),
and they also took some meat (food).*
Acts 27:34-36

DAY 5 INSTRUCTIONS:
Eat good stuff.

Eat something healthy today. If you already eat
healthy food, keep eating it today. Drink the
appropriate amount of water today. There are so
many resources on this subject. You can find
suggestions on the internet, in magazines, TV talk
shows, or call some government health department
or ask a friend. No excuses today. Okay?

What you put into your body reflects your love for you. Yes, it is more complicated than that, however, there is an element of truth to this. Can you make the extra effort today to eat something healthier than you "normally" eat? Sure you can. You need to energize your cells to get through the rest of the days of love.

Did you know that when a person is under a lot of stress, sometimes he or she may eat too much and others may eat too little? In Acts 27, as cited earlier, Paul and others were on a ship during a storm. They had good reason to fear for their lives through an imminent shipwreck. Yet, Paul asked them to eat because he knew they would be safe. That was probably the last thing on the sailors' minds. We sometimes have to slow down and think, "I'm safe in Jesus' hands. I will get through this difficult time and still eat healthy." Do you want to develop a new habit of loving yourself enough to slow down, think, plan and follow healthy eating habits?

If you've developed some unhealthy old habits, it will take you more than a day to change them. However, every journey begins with the first step: a goal or vision. How do you see where you want to be in your eating habits? Imagery is especially important in this area. Some diet advisors have you start with a current "before" picture of yourself. If you do, hide it someplace in a drawer or box. Get a before the before picture of yourself when you were slim and trim. If it doesn't exist, take the slimmest picture you've got and have a photo enhancer technician digitally slim you down. Stare at that every day. Find a diet book or plan, approved by your doctor that appeals to you.

Find a user-friendly healthy eating program. So, without further ado, go to it. Plan something healthy. I'm sure you will think of something nice and nutritional. Take one bite at a time!

EAT FOR YOUR HEALTH AND WELL BEING.
Suggestions on how to complete this day:
1. Eat fruit.
2. Eat green and yellow (orange) vegetables.
3. Drink water.
4. Avoid refined sugar.
5. Avoid white flour products.
6. Eat slower, putting that fork down in between bites.
7. Write down what you are eating today.

You could also do the above in a group, like a church gathering, "party" or a simple family meal. Just remember to plan for the other 20 hours in the day, when you are not at the gathering. However you get through this day, find something or some way to make it happen. If you look, you will find. You can eat healthy for today.

How I ate what was good for me today:

13

DAY SIX:
Work Out

*I beseech you therefore, brethren, by the
mercies of God, that ye present your bodies a
living sacrifice, holy acceptable unto God,
which is your reasonable (rational) service.
And be not conformed to this world; but be ye
transformed by the renewing of your mind,
that ye may prove what is that good, and
acceptable, and perfect, will of God.*
Romans 12:1-2

DAY 6 INSTRUCTIONS:
Work Your Body

Keeping your body fit, through regular exercises,
can have a mind-renewing affect on your attitude
and mental well-being as well. Therefore, let's do
physical exercise today. Be sure you have checked
with your doctor to approve of your exercise plan.

During Biblical times, people walked to get
water, walked to get to the synagogue. They even
walked for miles and days, just to pay their taxes.
If they wanted entertainment at the amphitheater,

they walked to it and up and down the stairs of the coliseum because there were no elevators. Today, we have remote control for our TVs.

We have to make exercise a priority by scheduling it into our day. People with limited mobility have sometimes been taught how to exercise sitting down and while lying in bed. No excuses. If you can hold this book and read it, you can do something. Today, move those arms, legs and torso to the full extent allowed. Do what is comfortable for you without hurting yourself. Get off the couch. Use that remote control and can of beverage as hand bells, if you can't pull yourself away from the TV. Move those arms up and down. Doesn't that feel good?

Move your body!
One, two, three, four,
five, six, seven, eight,
nine, ten.
Once again now!

If you have limbs that move, what a blessing. Show your love to you and appreciation to the Lord by taking care of your temple (your body).

GET IN SHAPE FOR SERVICE.
Suggestions on how to complete this day:

1. Spend part of your lunch break walking.

2. Move your legs and arms up and down, while sitting and working at your desk.

3. Go to the gym that you have a membership in. Use some of the fancy machines that monitor how many calories you are using up, heartbeat, time and distance covered (stationary aerobic fitness equipment).

4. Walk up and down your home stairs a few times.

5. Invite a friend, mate or your child to exercise with you today.

6. Take a brisk walk through the mall.

7. Churches can invite a fitness trainer to demonstrate to attendees how to exercise safely.

Love your body!

How I exercised today:

_____

14

DAY SEVEN:
Think

*This book of the law shall not depart
out of thy mouth (shall be constantly
in); but thou shalt meditate therein day
and night, that thou mayest observe to
do according to all that is written
therein: for then thou shalt make thy
way prosperous, and then thou shall
have good success.*
Joshua 1:8

DAY 7 INSTRUCTIONS:
Think about Him and what He wants you to learn today

It is time to nourish your spiritual soul. Read your Bible. Look up a subject in a concordance, which is found in the back of most Bibles, and study something of interest to you. Set aside 30 to 60 minutes of quiet time, alone, no noise and distractions, when you can communicate with the Lord. Just as important, allow the Lord to communicate with you. Write your thoughts and

His directions down. You are a spiritual soul. This is the day to get in touch with it.

Set aside a quiet time and read a good book that is educational or inspirational. Stop, think and reflect on how it can make your life better. It could be the Bible, but could also be another book.

Techies can read the Bible from affordable software that usually contains several versions. Audio people can hear the Bible in its entirety on CD's. That way, you can hear the Bible while riding in your car, probably in less than a year, without taking any time away from your other responsibilities. Try handheld, digital book readers, tablets, smart phones, PCs and PDA's, when you want to read the Bible on the go. Whatever works for you, allow some quiet time to digest, reflect, and hear with your heart (as well as your mind) what thus saith the Lord.

MEDITATE DAY AND NIGHT
Suggestions on how to complete this day:

1. Find a quiet time and with pen and paper, over a 30-60 minute timeframe, write your concerns and then God's response to what you should do.

2. Read one or two chapters in the Bible, put it down, and reflect on what that passage means to you.

3. Go to a quiet place, with a beautiful view of nature, and just listen to God's voice.

4. Walk around (in a safe place) and think about your life and what is important to you. Ask God to point you in the right direction.

5. Make no pre-judgment on what God is going to tell you to do or not do today. Observe throughout the day how it unfolds with fewer surprises.

6. Enter in a notebook, computer or hand-held device, words of inspiration and encouragement for achieving your purpose and goals in life.

7. In a group, ask a thought-provoking question. Have volunteers respond. For example, "How do my personal goals reflect love for myself, others and God?"

How I meditated on the Lord today:

15

DAY EIGHT:
Hug

*In that hour Jesus rejoiced in spirit, and said,
I thank thee, O Father, Lord of heaven and
earth, that thou hast hid these things from the
wise and prudent, and hast revealed them
unto babes; even so, Father, for so it seemed
good in thy sight.*
Luke 10:21

DAY 8 INSTRUCTIONS:
Hug You, Faults, and All

Knowledge is so vast that the smartest person in the world knows less than a speck of sand compared to what there is to know in the universe.

The scripture in Luke 10 cited earlier, may seem like an unlikely selection to remind us to hug ourselves, faults and all. However, it points out by illustration that no matter how great, powerful, and rich we become, God determines what we know. God can reveal and withhold critical information for our survival, regardless of our status in society's eyes. This passage can be considered to be the "great equalizer" clause. We are going to have faults and make mistakes. Nevertheless, we can rejoice and hug ourselves anyway. If we are saved by grace, our names are written in heaven. Our sins are wiped away, forever forgotten by God.

Jesus highlighted in Luke 10 that no matter what kind of miraculous healing powers the disciples had, not to get a big head about it. Have no illusion that you are infallible, or worse, the smartest kid on the block, just because you got all "A's" or have an impressive title. There will always be someone out there who knows something that you do not know. And that other person might just call that mistake you made to your attention in front of a TV camera, for instance. Sure you will feel embarrassed, angry or depressed about it. Making mistakes is part of life.

Failure in something is inevitable and is a vital part of learning. Give yourself a break. Be kind to yourself. Learn and move on. Just don't keep doing the same mistake over and over. Only God knows enough to never make a mistake. In fact, according to Luke 10, God deliberately withholds some information from the wise and gives it to the uneducated and untitled (babes).

A major reason people don't like themselves is because of the mistakes they've made. Human mistakes are part of God's plan to bring you closer to Him. If you never made a mistake, you wouldn't need God. Some people feel so guilty about making a mistake that it nearly paralyzes them from moving forward. Wash your hands free of guilt (figuratively speaking). No matter what your accomplishments (earning a doctorate's degree, winning a Nobel Peace Prize, healing the sick, etc), the most important thing is that your name be written in heaven. You can have that with Jesus' blessings.

Give yourself a big hug for that!

EVEN IF YOU DON'T KNOW EVERYTHING, KNOW GOD.

Suggestions on how to complete this day:

1. Stand and take a towel to help you wrap your arms around your chest reaching towards the back to hug yourself.

2. Lay on your back, pull your bent legs up to your chest, and wrap your arms around your legs, giving yourself a big hug.

3. Sit on the floor, with bended knees up to your chest and hug yourself.

4. Close your eyes and visualize a picture of you hugging yourself.

5. If hugging yourself is truly not your thing, reach your right hand over your left shoulder, and give yourself a quick pat on the back when no one is looking.

6. Groups can stand in a circle (or line) and cross their right arms over their left arms (provides a front body hug), hold hands and sing, "Jesus Loves Me," or another spiritually uplifting song.

7. Mates can hug each other, while whispering sweet words in each other's ear, like, "Love Yourself."

How I accepted my failures and hugged myself today:

_____

16

DAY NINE:
Create

Neglect not the gift that is in thee...
1 Timothy 4:14

DAY 9 INSTRUCTIONS:
Make something new to show your love for you.

You are a creature, created by God to create something. Otherwise, He wouldn't have had any need to create you. When you were told to "Do this" or "Not that way," or "Be quiet," or "Speak up," it was so easy to just follow orders. There is a time to follow orders from those people who have authority over you. There is also a time to forge new paths, and follow God's order to be creative in order to achieve your God-given vision.

Because God made you unique, He has also provided a time for you to use your gifts for a unique purpose. You were made to be creative by the Creator. Ask God what He wants you to create. Be flexible. Go with God's flow.

Be a little different today. Remind yourself that you were created for a purpose that only you can fulfill. If you focus on how to be creative in love, you can do it. Sometimes, just breaking a routine gets your creative thoughts flowing and opens up a new way of thinking and doing things.

YOU HAVE BEEN GIVEN DOMINION OVER THE EARTH.
DO SOMETHING WITH IT, IN LOVE.
Suggestions on how to complete this day:

1. Write a story about your life in one short paragraph.

2. Make yourself a positive affirmation index card, using multiple-color markers. (Example, "I am uniquely created. "Jesus loves my creativity, because that's part of me.")

3. Start a family scrapbook, as a memory keepsake for you and your family.

4. Take a scenic drive in your area, in a route that you've never taken before, with your mate or close friend. Note and discuss new thoughts along the way.

5. Rearrange you desk or dresser top, to clear your view of clutter and distractions.

6. Groups can share drawing a giant get-well greeting card and donate it to a children's hospital ward.

7. Explore some of the software tools that are already on computers to create a new graphic design for inspiration.

How I created something new today:

17

DAY TEN:
Relax

*And the apostles gathered themselves together
unto Jesus, and told him all things, both what
they had done, and what they had taught.
And he said unto them, Come ye yourselves apart
(aside) into a desert (deserted) place and rest a
while; for there were many coming and going, and
they had no leisure so much as to eat.
And they departed into a desert (deserted)
place by ship privately (by themselves).*
Mark 6:30, 31, 32

DAY 10 INSTRUCTIONS:
Relax

There are times when the best part of living is doing nothing but sitting and taking it all in. Stop to smell the roses. Stop to hear God's voice. Enjoy the moment as presented, because the present will never return. Slow down to watch and access where you are now. Slow down and focus on what God is telling you through this beautiful world He created. You've worked hard to make it to this day. Take a load off your feet. Some of the most insightful moments can be when one is sitting still or lying down. Young Samuel, a prophet of Israel, was lying down to sleep when God called to give him a prophesy or vision. (I Samuel 3:9, 10)

Sometimes God comes to us in a whisper. (I Kings 19) Such was the case of Elijah, who was under great stress as the result of fleeing from Jezebel, King Ahab's wife, because he did not bow to Baal, a false god. She had threatened to kill him. The stress was so high that Elijah just wanted to die. So he went to the wilderness and sat under a tree, asking the Lord to take his life. However, God had a way to reach him in love.

God's voice was not in the wind, earthquake or fire. It was in a small still whisper. Only after Elijah was comforted with food, rested and quiet, did God assure him that he was not alone. Soon thereafter, God directed Elijah to anoint a new prophet, Elisha, who ministered unto him. (I Kings 19-19-21)

God will minister unto you in time of need if you will just slow down and take the time to hear and receive His help. God knows when you are tired and worn down from the struggles of life. He knows when you need rest and help. Many times, He will give you a sign through physical symptoms that warn you to rest. Pay attention to them.

Some people from the moment they wake up, until the moment they are in bed, need to have either the radio or TV or audio player with earplugs on all day long. You need time, including during your awake hours, to relax quietly so that you can hear a word from the Lord, even if it is in a whisper.

The body needs time to rejuvenate. You were designed by God to rest on a regular basis. Jesus knew it was important to teach, preach, heal and lead people into the "Christian" way and to save the whole world in just a few years. This was not easy. He rested anyway. Remember, Jesus found time. He also instructed His 12 apostles to get away from the crowd and rest a while. (Mark 6:31)

You can't give what you do not have. If you are tired and run down from running here and there, including helping others in ministries, eventually you will run down in your ability to help others as well as you would like. Slow down today.

If you can't relax one day or hour out of 21 days, then you are too busy and may need to rearrange your schedule.

GIVE YOURSELF A BREAK TODAY
Suggestions on how to complete this day:

1. Schedule and write at least 30 minutes to an hour or two on your calendar to "do absolutely nothing."

2. Spend a day or hour or two at a spa.

3. Inform your family not to disturb you for an hour or two. (It can be done.)

4. Go to a park or scenic area and quietly relax while taking in the view. (Make sure it is a safe place.)

5. As a group, spend a mealtime, eating, smiling, but no speaking, no TV or radio background music. Some churches have done this during Maundy Thursday of the Holy Week.

6. For couples, spend an hour in quiet meditation together. No touching.

7. For techies, this day can be very difficult. Turn the cell phone off. Do not check to see if you missed a call. No text messaging. No computer usage. No video and electronic games. Try this for at least an hour.

How I relaxed today:

PART III

Love Outside

18

DAY ELEVEN:
Give Greetings

*Finally, brethren, farewell, Be perfect, be of
one mind, live in peace; and the God of love
and peace shall be with you.
Greet one another with an holy kiss.
All the saints salute (greet) you.
The grace of the Lord Jesus Christ, and the
love of God, and the communion (fellowship)
of the Holy Ghost, be with you all. Amen.*
2 Corinthians 13:11-14

DAY 11 INSTRUCTIONS:
Greet Someone with a Blessed Day

Now that you have loved yourself for ten days in
a row, get ready to love others! Practice turning the
love within you, outward to others. The Apostle
Paul was a big figure, in terms of what we would
view today as social status. When Paul talked,
people listened. Yet, he warned his listeners of not
being boastful of self accomplishments as though
they did this all by themselves. (2 Corinthians 10)
Paul was also a "war hero," having been beaten and

put in prison for preaching about Christ. (2 Corinthians 11:23-26) One group of people, on the island of Melita, thought and said he was a god. (Acts 28:6) This "larger-than-life" image of Paul did not deter him from thinking of others' well-being. Paul realized that he was not the main attraction.

Begin this day with an uplifting greeting as you encounter people along the way. When you get up in the morning, tell the people in your household, "Good morning! Hope you have a great day today." As you rush to work, passing strangers along the way, smile and greet them with a, "Have a blessed day." When you arrive to school, or work, the spa, or shopping trip, tell them, "Good to see you. Hope all is well for you today." Give them a smile. Say, "Hello" to the parking attendant, security guard, janitor and gardener. Say, "Hello. How are you feeling today?" to the grocery clerk or gas station attendant, before they do. Be a one-person customer service greeter for Christ. You never know if someone is having a bad day or feeling down. You may be the only person that day who has words of kindness for them. Think about how you feel when someone gives you a similar greeting.

Greetings are not just for beginning your days. At the end of the day, when settling in for the night with your family, give them an evening greeting like, "Sleep tight. God loves you with all His might." Throw in a kiss or hug.

HI. GOOD TO SEE YOU.

Suggestions on how to complete this day:

1. Any of the suggestions cited earlier.

2. Have a greeting on your signature line for emails and letters and text messages.

3. You can send greeting cards by email, telephone, or deliver in person.

4. Speak other greetings like, "Be blessed." or "Wishing you God's grace today!"

5. Greet in peace by saying, "Peace, brother (or sister)."

6. In a group, tell the person next to you, "Have a blessed day."

7. Learn to say a greeting in a foreign language such as Arabic, Chinese, French, German, Hebrew, Japanese, Russian, Spanish or Swahili, etc. (Look them up in a translation dictionary or on the internet.)

How I greeted someone with a "Have a blessed day." today:

19

DAY TWELVE:
Chat

*And after the reading of the law and the
prophets the rules of the synagogue sent unto
them, saying, Ye men and brethren, if ye have
any word of exhortation for the people, say on.
Then Paul stood up, and beckoning with his
hand said, Men of Israel, and ye that fear
God, give audience.*
Acts 13:15, 16

DAY 12 INSTRUCTIONS:
Have a chat

It is not so common now. However, people used
to "chat" by writing each other letters back and
forth. Going to the mailbox and finding a
handwritten letter from a friend or love one was
usually very uplifting. Sometimes people would
hold and study the envelope before opening it,
perhaps noticing a perfumed scent that had been
thoughtfully added to the stationary. Letter delivery
in Biblical times could take days and weeks because

there was no "overnight air delivery" option. Nor was there a telephone to dial.

Today, we can just pick up a telephone and chat or text message someone. Any way you can do a special chat is special to the recipient, whether they acknowledge it or not. Some people truly have the gift of gab. If you are not one of those persons, don't let that stop you from reaching out in simple words.

Unfortunately, not everyone will appreciate your friendly conversations. When you do right, like speaking up for Jesus, some people are going to be jealous and try to put a lot of stress on you. Note the Apostle Paul's ordeal when he spoke up for the Lord. (Acts 14) Having a support system like friends and family is essential to maintaining your composure and confidence under duress. That is why it is important to reach out and be a friend so when you need a friend, someone will be there for you. We need friends and family just as much during successful times as during our failing moments.

Call a friend or family member to chat and give him or her words of encouragement. If you are at work, or a social gathering, reach out and befriend someone with a little chitchat. Express your interest in what they are doing, saying, or wearing. Give sincere compliments. Talk about "nothing." Just be there for that person at that moment in his or her life.

By "losing yourself" in the other person's current concerns, you often "find yourself" through a different perspective. God's messages to us can come in a variety of ways. Befriending others may be just another avenue for God to give you something.

Open up and listen carefully by being an active listener. "Active listening" refers to hearing what the other person is saying by responding through verbal and non-verbal gestures (body language) in a way that lets them know that you heard and understood them correctly. This may be through empathy and rephrasing their words, as well as asking for their feedback, to see if you received their message correctly. It sometimes requires clarification, verification, and supportive responses to fully understand them. A good active listener, who gives love, feels the warmth of that love come right back to them from the other person being listened to.

SAY ON, BROTHERS AND SISTERS:
Suggestions on how to complete this day:

1. Invite someone to lunch.

2. Invite someone to dinner.

3. Invite someone to breakfast.

4. Initiate a short chat with a co-worker at break-time.

5. Skype someone when you have time to "chat" back and forth together.

6. Call someone on the phone.

7. Text message someone for a chat (only if it is on your personal device, and not the company's.)

How I chatted with someone today:

20

DAY THIRTEEN:
Break Bread

*And they continued steadfastly in the apostles'
doctrine and fellowship, and in breaking of
bread, and in prayers.
And they, continuing daily with one accord
(mind) in the temple, and breaking bread from
house to house, did eat their meat (food) with
gladness and singleness (simplicity) of heart.*
Acts 2:42, 46

DAY 13 INSTRUCTIONS:
Break bread with someone.

We all have this one thing in common: we have
to eat. It is not an option. It is required for survival.
Sharing a meal together provides a common ground
of interest and needs. We can use that factor to
bridge the gap in communications. One of the most
popular non-verbal acts of love is to treat the
guest/honoree to a special meal. Rich people have
been known to spend hundreds of thousands of
dollars on a dinner event to show their love for

someone. However, you can also make a big impression spending much less.

Weddings, anniversaries, birthdays and retirement celebrations, invariably include food. Why is that? It says, "I love you enough to feed you." Can you imagine going to a birthday party with no food?

Today, make eating a meal with someone a little special. Christ loved his followers enough to take time to feed thousands. (John 6:10, 11) If it was that important to Him to connect with others, it should be just as important to us.

If you don't cook, share a treat like fruit with someone. Offer them a morsel of bread, if that is all you have. The idea is to share something, hopefully nourishing. Do not wait for a special occasion to break bread with someone. Do it today. It just might be the best thing that happens to you and/or that person all day.

Techies can order food online from your cell phone to be delivered to a gathering that you will be attending. Groups can share potluck meals or cater a dinner. Add a special twist to what you might normally do.

SIT AND EAT.
Suggestions on how to complete this day:

1. Bring in some grapes or cherries in small paper cupcake holders, so people can pick them up and cart them back to their work desk.

2. If this is a sports event day or night, fix some finger food, like vegetable trays with healthy dips.

3. Make reservations at a new restaurant in town.

4. Find a new recipe to cook and share with family.

5. Cook someone their favorite dish.

6. Arrange a caterer to prepare a small meal and have it hand-delivered to your home or to that special person's home.

7. Stop by a deli, bakery, or food specialty shop where they sell cooked items by the pound. Get a little bit of many items for a small intimate smorgasbord.

How I shared healthy food with someone today:

_____

21

DAY FOURTEEN:
Donate

I have shewed you all things, how that so labouring ye ought to support the weak, and to remember the words of the Lord Jesus, how he said, It is more blessed to give than to receive.
And when he had thus spoken, he kneeled down, and prayed with them all.
And they all wept sore, and fell on Paul's neck, and kissed him.
Acts 20:35-37

DAY 14 INSTRUCTIONS:
Make a Donation

Have you ever seen a truly selfish, self-absorbed person? They are "always" looking for what they can get, with no interest in what they can give to others. They seem to be very unhappy people.

The reality is that there will always be someone else with more than you have, unless you are the richest person on earth. That makes for several billion unhappy people, if happiness was based on what one owns.

Now, let's flip the scenario. Have you noticed people who are generous, giving, and thoughtful of other's needs? They seem to be happier and less stressed out than the selfish group. Giving is receiving. In genuine heart-felt giving, it is not unusual to get back more than one gives from an entirely different source. Perhaps, since God seems to enjoy giving, He may be teaching us how to be happier by giving.

Most of us have too much stuff. When you get rid of the excess baggage in your life, you make room for new bags. This is a win-win. The charity gets the goods, while you may get a tax credit. Plus, all of your clutter is gone. It's been said that you can tell where a person's values are by looking at his or her checkbook log. Do you have at least one entry in your whole checkbook log to someone in need, charity or church, with no direct benefit to yourself? Whatever you give, make sure it is something of value. Do not give away true junk. However, you would be amazed at how an item that is trivial to you is a treasure to someone else.

JOYOUS GIVING
Suggestions on how to complete this day:

1. Walk around your home with an empty gift basket in tow. As you stroll through your rooms, look for something of value that you have not used in a long time. Place it in the basket (if it is too big, put a sticky note on it

that reads, "This is someone's gift." Once you have accumulated a few items in the gift basket, wrap it up with a pretty ribbon. Donate to someone or your favorite charity.

2. Write a check above the normal amount that you usually give for your church or favorite charity.

3. Donate your time at a non-profit agency for a day or evening.

4. Drop a few bills in the seasonal charity kettles or children's school fundraising event.

5. Give a homeless person a donation.

6. Select a favorite cause to ask others to donate to.

7. Donate to a college or university.

How I donated something today:

_____

22

DAY FIFTEEN:
Embrace

And Esau ran to meet him (Jacob), and
embraced him, and fell on his neck, and kissed
him; and they wept.
Genesis 33:4

DAY 14 INSTRUCTIONS:
Hug someone

Humans need the human touch to grow and develop from infancy. As adults, we never outgrow our need for some type of bodily contact. Of course, you have to watch out for the appearance of sexual harassment and other inappropriate touching.

There is a rather lengthy story in the book of Genesis about two brothers, Esau and Jacob. (Genesis Chapters 27, 28, 32 and 33) Jacob had gotten Esau's birthright, which resulted in Esau losing his family status as the eldest who was entitled to certain inheritances from their father Isaac. The animosity caused between the two brothers, as the result of this, resulted in Jacob fleeing from Esau and their homestead. Jacob was gone from his brother and father for over 20 years. How did they make amends after such a long absence? Jacob sent gifts of cattle to Esau as an appeasement. However, material gifts were not what truly brought the brothers together. It was love, which was not expressed in a thousand words of excuses and explanations. It was their hugs and kisses that brought tears of joy. (Genesis 33:4)

They had a family reunion, right there on the spot, catching up on all the missed years and new family members.

My point is that a hug and kiss from the heart can sometimes melt away decades of feuding and neglect. Try it today. Note the positive effect that such a wordless gesture can have on your relationship. It is absolutely amazing the beneficial effect that a parent's daily hugs will have on their child's behavior.

Also, you get an immediate return on your emotional investment through hugging others because, when you hug someone, they are typically simultaneously hugging you back. What a spiritual lift!

GIVE A HUG.
Suggestions on how to complete this day:

1. Hug a family member

2. At the urging of your pastor, if this is during Sunday Service, give someone a hug.

3. If you have no one to hug, hug your therapist.

4. Visit a nursing home. Ask the nurse if it is okay to hug someone in need of a hug.

5. If no one around you is the right candidate for a hug, text message or call someone up and give them an imaginary hug in writing or verbally. (Example, say or write, "Hugs and Kisses to You from Me!")

6. If that is not your thing, find a picture of a love one and spiritually hug it.

7. If you are still at a loss, give Jesus a big hug in your prayers.

How I hugged someone today:

_____

23

DAY SIXTEEN:
Do a Deed

For I was an hungered, and ye gave me meat; I was thirsty, and ye gave me drink; I was a stranger, and ye took me in;
Naked, and ye clothed me; I was sick, and ye visited me; I was in prison, and ye came unto me.
Then shall the righteous answer him, saying, Lord, when saw we thee an hungered, and fed thee: or thirst, and gave thee drink:
When saw we thee a stranger, and took thee in? Or naked, and clothed thee?
Or when saw we thee sick, or in prison and came unto thee?
And the King shall answer and say unto them, Verily I say unto you, Inasmuch as ye have done it unto one of the least of these my brethren, ye have done it unto me.
Matthew 25:35-40

DAY 16 INSTRUCTIONS:
Do a household chore for a love one.

If ever there was a time to help others, this is it. Due to the economy, many people have lost their homes. Many are unemployed or underemployed. From time to time, we all need help of some sort. It is tempting to "ignore" the suffering of others. However, today, please think of them and what you can do to help them. None of us have gotten where we are without the help of others. It may have been a lift to school when you couldn't drive. If we all pitched in a little today, what a big difference our world would be.

Helping others with mundane chores is not glamorous. It is often a thankless job. But we must do it if we want to emulate Jesus. Jesus reminded us in Matthew 25 earlier, that when you help the needy, you help Him. When you spiritually go before Him, He will remember your good deeds, even if no one else notices.

People who need your services are often hesitant to ask for it; or their minds have deteriorated and they don't know what to ask for. Then there are others who would be very resentful, (out of denial that their home is in shambles) that you would offer to do a household chore. With those caveats in mind, use God's guidance on whom to offer your services. Do it with thanksgiving and gladness. Just pretend that you are washing Jesus' floors. Imagine that you've been especially picked to wash Jesus' dishes.

If you do not have someone in your home who you can do this for, find a relative or friend who could use a little break in this area. It may be something as simple as changing the toilet paper roll, hanging fresh towels, or taking the dirty clothes basket to the laundry room. While you are at it, sort the clothes.

If you are at work, you can volunteer to temporarily relieve a co-worker of that unpleasant task of cleaning the coffee maker. It may be answering the phones so that they can get a task done with less interruption.

People helped you in the past. Sometimes, it is so minor that you may not remember it. Additionally, it will usually give you a lift also. One day, someone may offer to help you in a jam. However, the main reason you do this is to show your love for others. Take a load off someone today.

WHEN YOU HELP OTHERS, YOU HELP JESUS.

Suggestions on how to complete this day:

1. Wash dishes when it is not your turn.

2. Wash clothes for someone who can't do it because of physical confinement.

3. Clean someone's floors and carpets.

4. Buy and deliver groceries and toiletries for someone on a fixed income.

5. Take a duster and wipe the dust off the furniture.

6. As a group, give an extra cleaning to your church or charity place.

7. For techies, show someone how to use a command on a cell phone or computer.

How I helped someone in need today:

_____

24

DAY SEVENTEEN:
Visit

Is any among you afflicted (suffering)? let him pray.
Is any merry (cheerful)? let him sing psalms.
Is any sick among you? let him call for the elders
of the church; and let them pray over him,
anointing him with oil in the name of the Lord:
And the prayer of faith shall save the sick, and
the Lord shall raise him up; and if he has
committed sins, they shall be forgiven him.
Confess you faults (trespasses) one to another,
and pray one for another, that ye may be healed.
The effectual (effective) fervent prayer
(supplication) of a righteous man availeth much.
James 5:13-16

DAY 17 INSTRUCTIONS:
Call or Visit A Sick or Homebound Person and Pray with Them

Sometimes a person can go for decades without a single close family member dying or becoming disabled to the extent of requiring 24-hour care. Then, just as possible, several close family members and friends can pass away within a short time period. The suffering your love ones may have endured before the end can be just as difficult to take as the passing. Then there are older relatives who need daily care, as they are not likely to get better over time.

Many of us have this hope that when/if we get sick, we will make a full recovery. The reality is that we are mortals. We are born; we live varied lives; and then we die. This is a hard pill to swallow at any stage of life.

Don't let the sick and homebound go through this "normal" passage of human existence alone. Visit them. Sit down, chat. Don't be in a hurry. They have today, but maybe not tomorrow. Listen to their words of wisdom. There is nothing more likely to be coming out of a man or woman that is facing the end of his or her road than truthfulness. Hopefully, when you leave from that visit you will appreciate more of the "little things" in life that so many of us "able-bodied" take for granted. Just having the ability to leave that place on your own freewill and walk outside feeling the warm sun or chilled snowflakes on your face is an experience not independently possible for millions on this earth. Cherish each breath you take. Don't squander them on nonsense. One day it will be your last.

If you find it too confining to visit for an hour or two with a shut-in or terminally ill person, just try to imagine how they must feel to be stuck in the same old place indefinitely. Go with a friend or family member, if that will help.

Pastors and other ministers and chaplains can't take care of every sick or shut-in person. Unfortunately, there are so many ill people. Recent years of hurricanes, floods, earthquakes, typhoons and other natural disasters, have increased the need for help. Relatives are often over-extended, out of town, or just not interested. It is Biblical to visit the sick. Find a way. No excuses. If you miss this day, remember you have to start all over back to day one. However, if your schedule does not permit, you can switch this day with another day's instruction in this book. Sending things, or money, just isn't enough here. Be seen by them and God helping others. Reach out to the sick or shut-in today. As we get older, there will be more of us in that category.

Many similar issues pertain to prisoners and their families. Remember them in a meaningful way. You can fulfill today's habit of love by helping either the sick, shut in, homebound, prisoner, or prisoner's family.

BE A PRAYER PARTNER
Suggestions on how to complete this day:

1. Visit a sick family member or friend.

2. Visit someone in a nursing home. If you don't know of a sick person, contact a nursing home and request that the staff give permission for you to visit someone who would appreciate getting a visit from you. More elderly than you think have no one who regularly visits them.

3. Visit a prisoner, or his or her family.

4. Take the sick or shut-in person to the doctor or for a ride around town so they can see what is being built or torn down in the community.

5. Have delivered, or bring, a hot, nutritious meal to a shut-in person. Stay to eat with them. Clean up afterwards.

6. Audio tape and/or video tape a message of wisdom or family history from the shut-in or prisoner to give to family members.

7. Send a cell-phone snapshot or video of the shut-in person to send to other family members, and share family news with your sick and shut-in family members.

How I called or visited the sick or shut-in today:

_____

25

DAY EIGHTEEN:
Thank

*And one of them (out of the 10 lepers that
Christ healed), when he saw that he was
healed, turned back, and with a loud voice
glorified God,
And fell down on his face at his feet, **giving
him thanks**; and he was a Samaritan.
And Jesus answering, said, Were there not ten
cleansed: but where are the nine?
There are not found that returned to give
glory to God, save this stranger.
And he said unto him, Arise, go thy way: thy
faith hath made thee whole.*
Luke 17:15-19

DAY 18 INSTRUCTIONS:
Send A Thank-You Card

The words, "thank-you" and "please" were
among the first etiquette lessons a toddler learned.
Most of us automatically say, "thank you," while
receiving something pleasant. On the other hand,
relatively few of us go the extra mile to write and

mail a thank-you for nice things people have done for us, unless it is a special occasion like weddings and showers.

Often, our society does not expect us to write a thank-you note for a regular/non-special event. What a pleasant surprise to the recipient if they got a note of gratitude and thanks from you. When you send such a note, especially when the person is not expecting it, you let them know that you noticed what they did. When you think of them, they think of you. Just as important, God notices too. What you do in a "quiet" note of thanks will be rewarded by God well beyond the cost of stationary.

Write and give a thank-you note to someone. If you don't have anyone to send it to, write one for God.

BE THE ONE OUT OF TEN
Suggestions on how to complete this day:

1. Buy a special thank-you greeting card to send. (Some have music and can record your voice.)

2. Make your own hand-made, thank-you card, out of colorful paper and ink markers.

3. Personalize a thank-you by painting a picture and having the card framed.

4. Send a thank-you greeting card by internet or text message.

5. Verbally, send a sweet thank-you poem. Leave it on the person's voice mail.

6. Hire someone to give a verbal and visual thank-you message.

7. Lease a billboard with a thank-you message from a group to a special person/agency, or group.

How I sent a thank-you card today:

_____

26

DAY NINETEEN:
Love

He that loveth his brother abideth in the light,
and there is no occasion of (no cause for)
stumbling in him.
1 John 2:10

DAY 19 INSTRUCTIONS:
Tell someone, preferably your significant
other, "I love you."

If ever there was a time to be genuine and
sincere, it is when you say, "I love you." What's so
special about those three little words? When you
use them, you are also saying to the other person,
"You are lovable." You affirm what God already
knows. He shows love to us every day of our lives.
If no one else loves you, God does. People need to
be reminded that they are loved, even when they
mess up in life. Seize the moment to tell someone
you love them. Your life will be much richer for it.
Truly, if you reap what you sow, this is the place to
sow your seeds of love.

Jesus included as the commandment to love among the two most important commandments to follow. (Matthew 22:36-40) What better way to express love than to say the actual words, "I love you." and mean it from your heart?

Notice the word "love" is in between the "I" and "you." It is the great connector between people. It is what life is all about. It brings meaning to relationships. Love is living life fully.

Say to your child, lover, or family the specific words, "I love you?"

If you are not used to saying those words to someone, it can be difficult. Write it on a piece of paper to give someone or say it through a greeting card. (Do this in addition to birthday, Valentine and anniversary cards, if you normally send cards on those occasions.) This is a "I love you for no special event" communication. Leave it in the other person's car, so that they see it just before going to work, for example.

Some people would rather buy a love one a physical gift like jewelry or take them out to dinner or fancy vacations, than say, "I love you." However, there is no real substitute for the words, "I love you." You might get by with a million dollar diamond ring, but it is not identical. The recipient might even prefer the ring over the words, but that is another matter.

What if you don't love anyone at this time? Da! This book is about love. You've made it this far to the nineteenth day. It's time to find somebody to love. If in your heart you really don't love someone else today, *act* like you love someone. This may help you to feel it in your heart eventually. Say, "I love you," silently to yourself, to get in practice.

For the truly anxious, and as a last resort, drastic is more like it, do the following:

Explain to someone that you are reading this book, *21 Days of Love*, and to complete the 19th day's instructions properly, you have to tell someone that you love them like a brother or sister. Then ask their permission if they would mind if you said, "I love you," to them.

After your lengthy explanation, they may either give you permission (out of love for you, or pity) or think you are crazy for asking. Either way, you've said, "I love you" in your explanation and can move on to day 20. Was that helpful? ☺

LOVE HAS NO EXCUSES.
Suggestions on how to complete this day:

1. When she is shopping or he is looking at a sports game, say with a smile, "I love you." For the shopper, say this when traveling between stores. For the sports fan, say it during time outs or breaks in play.

2. Say it before your mate showers, shaves or puts on make-up.

3. Just say it in person. Almost anytime is good.

4. Send a short video of you saying, "I love you."

5. E-mail or text a friend or family member in your household.

6. Buy a greeting card that allows you to record the words, "I love you."

7. Leave a message on the answering machine saying, "I love you."

How I told someone "I love you" today:

_____

27

DAY TWENTY:
Give

Give, and it shall be given unto you; good measure, pressed down, and shaken together, and running over, shall men give into your bosom (The fold in a garment used as a pocket). For with the same measure that ye mete withal (use) it shall be measured to you again.
Luke 6:38

DAY 21 INSTRUCTIONS:
Give a Gift to Someone You Love for No Reason

Sometimes people need a "sign" that you appreciate them or, better yet, love them. Some people say, "I love you" a lot, but don't show it in any way, making the words meaningless.

While material things have their limitations, they can serve a purpose. We all have physical needs such as water, food, shelter and sleep. Once our basic survival and safety needs are met, we look to another human need: The need to be loved by others. One of the easiest ways to show your love is to give a person a gift, if only a small token gift. Gifts can say, "I'm thinking of you in a loving way." They add a sense of belonging to the giver and recipient. This is all relative. Don't be cheap with a cheap gift, if you can afford to give more.

Watch a child's eyes light up when you give him or her a gift, no matter how modest. Adults may try to hide that same enthusiasm, but when it comes to a free and clear gift, our hearts light up also.

Not that you need this to give, but the scripture does state that when you give it shall be given back to you in even greater quantity than you gave. (Luke 6:38)

This should be a relatively easy step. No words required. In fact, no special occasion either. The goal is to make someone feel special because you thought enough of them to give them a gift.

If you like, use a little creativity. Just be sure it is covered with something, so that they have to open or unwrap it to see what is inside. If it is a new car, a bow will do.

Just a reminder, it is not the cost of the gift that really matters. Jesus noted the offering from the poor widow who gave little in cents, but more in spirit, than those with much greater financial resources. (Mark 12:41-44) It is the thought from the heart that counts. Most people like to receive gifts, especially for no reason. They may have complained about it, but they still liked getting something. For maximum effect, make sure your words match your actions through this token of love. Give in the spirit of love, peace and harmony.

WHEN GIVING IS GETTING
Suggestions on how to complete this day:

1. Give someone a copy of this book (not this copy), *21 Days of Love.*

2. Give a gift certificate that can be used in many different stores.

3. Ask someone to help you select a special gift. Give that helper a gift also.

4. Give your employees a bonus. If you are an employee, give your boss a gift.

5. Give an "I owe you" task certificate to be performed by you.

6. Give two tickets to a special entertainment or sporting event.

7. For the techies, give a flash drive (thumb drive), or tablet.

How I gave a gift to someone for no special reason today:

_____

28

DAY TWENTY-ONE: *Receive*

As the Father hath love me, so have I loved you; continue ye in my love.
John 15:9

DAY 21 INSTRUCTIONS:
Receive God's and Others' Gifts of Love.

There is no better gift in the world, than God's love for us. He made the ultimate sacrifice of sending His son, Jesus Christ, to die for us so that we may have everlasting life. (John 3:16) The Holy Bible is full of His many expressions of love. To name just a few, He gave us:

1. Liberty (Romans 8:21)

2. Joint-heirs with Christ (Romans 8:15-17)

3. Deliverance from evil works (II Timothy 4:18)

4. Peace (Isaiah 55:12)

5. Renewed Strength (Isaiah 40:31)

6. Salvation (Luke 19:10)

7. The Comforter (John 14:16)

God's love is like a circle. He loves us over and over again. (John 15:9-12) In turn, He asks that we love others. Take note of not only God's expressions of love, but also how others love us. Sometimes, we take the people closest to us for granted. Receive God's love and theirs graciously. Acknowledge their expressions of love with thanks and appreciation. They really did not "have to" show acts of kindness to you. You may be surprised to notice that there is a lot of love around you.

Collectively, the more people who engage in 21 consecutive days of love at the same time, the greater we can expand the circle of love.

RECEIVE LOVE GLADLY.

Suggestions on how to complete this day:

Write down how God and others expressed their love to you today and how you received them.

_____

_____

_____

_____

_____

_____

_____

What happens after the 21st Day?

Start all over at day one. Continue through the next 21 days, and the next, and the next. What a mental picture! At that rate, you will have love for the rest of your life.

Congratulations!

Conclusion

You have sown seeds of love for the past 21 days or more. You have given from your heart the most important gift you could give anyone...love. Did you know that every loving gift you give is from God?

Every good gift and every perfect gift is from above, and comes down from the Father of lights, with whom there is no variation or shadow of turning.
James 1:17

Always remember, the greatest gift of all was God's gift of His Son so that you could live. *"By grace you have been saved through faith, and not of yourselves; it is the gift of God"* (Ephesians 2:8). Live your life in the spirit in which it was given: lovingly.

After you have practiced going through the *21 Days of Love*, reflect back on which ones you enjoyed the most. Also, note if the recipients of your love enjoyed one expression of love more than others. Do more of that with them and yourself. With practice, you can get better and better at love. Keep giving love the next 21 days, and the next, and the next. Start a journal continually adding new and fresh ideas on loving self and others.

Use your experiences from the past 21 days to teach others the habit of love. Share your suggestions with others so that they will also know how to have love for 21 days.

You've achieved something great in life. This is the best habit anyone could have. It is the little things that can make a big difference when done in love. May you continue to be blessed for the next 21 days and beyond. Know that your acts of love reap acts of love by others over and over.

Last, but not least, the most important thing to remember about love is that when it is from the heart you will find a way to turn love inside out...today and every day.

Wouldn't it be wonderful if millions more people would practice the habit of love? Please share some of your creative habits of love with us, so that everyone gains valuable tips on how to keep their habits of love fresh and fun. We would love to hear from you at www.PaversHomes.com.

Made in the USA
Charleston, SC
06 August 2013